The History of Islam

MASON CREST PUBLISHERS
PHILADELPHIA

Divisions Within Islam

The History of Islam

Islam in Europe

Islam, Law, and Human Rights

Islamic-Jewish Relations Before 1947

Islamic Festivals and Celebrations

The Monotheistic Religions: Judaism, Christianity, Islam

Islam in America

The Muslim World: An Overview

Radical Islam

The History of Islam

BARRY RUBIN

Editorial Consultants: Foreign Policy Research Institute, Philadelphia, PA

Mason Crest Publishers
370 Reed Road
Broomall, PA 19008
www.masoncrest.com

Printed and bound in the United States of America.

First printing

1 3 5 7 9 8 6 4 2

Library of Congress Cataloging-in-Publication Data

Rubin, Barry M.
The history of Islam / Barry Rubin.
p. cm. — (World of Islam)
ISBN 978-1-4222-0531-0 (hardcover)
ISBN 978-1-4222-0799-4 (pbk.)
1. Islam—History—Juvenile literature. 2. Islamic countries—History—Juvenile literature. I. Title.
BP50.R83 2006
297.09—dc22
2008053414

Photo Credits: 7: Used under license from Shutterstock, Inc.; 8: Used under license from Shutterstock, Inc.; 10: Used under license from Shutterstock, Inc.; 12: Abdullah Y. Al-Dobats/Saudi Aramco World/Padia; 16: U.S. Navy Photo by Photographer's Mate 1st Class Arlo K. Abrahamson; 17: Used under license from Shutterstock, Inc.; 20: © 2009 Jupiterimages Corporation; 22: U.S. Army Photo by Spc. Charles W. Gill/DoD; 25: Used under license from Shutterstock, Inc.; 26: Used under license from Shutterstock, Inc.; 27: © 2009 Jupiterimages Corporation; 29: Used under license from Shutterstock, Inc.; 33: © OTTN Publishing; 34: Library of Congress; 35: Used under license from Shutterstock, Inc.; 37: Courtesy Turkish Tourist Office; 41: Nik Wheeler/Saudi Aramco World/Padia; 42: Library of Congress; 44: UN Photo; 45: (left) UN Photo/Evan Schneider, (right) UN Photo; 47: Used under license from Shutterstock, Inc.; 48: Used under license from Shutterstock, Inc.; 51: Used under license from Shutterstock, Inc.; 52: UN Photo/Eskinder Debebe; 54: Department of Defense; 55: U.S. Navy Photo by Journalist 1st Class Preston Keres; 57: Used under license from Shutterstock, Inc.

Barry Rubin is director of the Global Research in International Affairs (GLORIA) Center of the Interdisciplinary University. He is editor of the *Middle East Review of International Affairs (MERIA) Journal.*

Table of Contents

Islam and the Prophet Muhammad

Islam is an international religion, and today there are about 1.5 billion Muslims worldwide. However, the origins of the religion are very much tied to the Arabian Peninsula, in what is today Saudi Arabia.

In the era when Islam was born, 1,400 years ago, the vast desert of Arabia was dotted with towns like Mecca and Medina. The space between these towns was populated by Bedouins, pastoral nomads organized into tribes whose livelihood depended on the grazing of their flocks. These nomadic people were polytheists, believing in many tribal gods. By the sixth century, Christianity had reached some of Arabia's tribes, and there were also Jews living in the towns. Both of these religions influenced the ideas of the broader population.

Islam was to bring such a revolutionary shift in Arabia, and in the regions its adherents would conquer later, that Muslims

Muslims walk around the Kaaba, an ancient shrine in Mecca. Islam requires every Muslim to make a ritual pilgrimage to Mecca at least once during his or her lifetime if physically and financially able to do so.

refer to the period before Islam as *al-jahiliyyah*—"the period of ignorance." Consequently, this era is seen as an illegitimate period from which contemporary Muslims should feel themselves cut off.

In the year 570, Muhammad ibn Abdallah was born in Mecca into the clan of Hashim, a relation of the powerful Quraish tribe. By the time Muhammad was six years old, both his parents had died. He was raised by several relatives. In his 20s, he became a trader and married Khadija, a wealthy widow many years older than himself. He later married several additional wives.

According to Muslim belief, in the year 610, when Muhammad was 40 years old, he went to a hillside just outside Mecca seeking solitude. There he was said to have had a revelation from the Angel Gabriel. Muslims believe that Gabriel told Muhammad that

As a merchant leading camel caravans between Mecca and Damascus during the early seventh century C.E., Muhammad was exposed to the beliefs of many religions, including Judaism and Christianity. The Prophet would later encourage Jews and Christians to accept the new faith that he preached, Islam.

he was to be the messenger of God. It was from this point that the religion of Islam began.

Muhammad's Message

Muhammad began to preach to people in Mecca. He spoke about God, whom he called Allah. He told people that they must submit to Allah—the word *Islam* itself means "submission" in Arabic and refers to submitting to the will of God. A group of believers began to follow Muhammad. Like Muslims today, they believed Muhammad to be the final prophet sent by God to humanity in all of history. While God had earlier sent prophets to other nations throughout history, such as Moses and Jesus, Muslims believed their followers had failed to live by God's word.

The message Muhammad brought was higher and more correct, it was claimed, since it was God's last word on all subjects. As a result, religions that came into existence before Islam are deemed inaccurate; those that arose after Islam are seen as even more illegitimate. Polytheistic religions were viewed as the most objectionable of all. Islam was, therefore, the only proper religion for humanity to follow.

Muslims believe that God's words to Muhammad were revealed to him throughout his life. When written down, they became known as the Qur'an, the holy book of Islam.

Muslims believe that the core message Muhammad preached was that of monotheism. This is also the central principle of the Qur'an. Muslims are taught that Allah is the only God, is omnipotent, and is eternal. Therefore, idolatry, which is known as *shirk*, is a sin. Muhammad also taught that Allah created the world but that the process of creation was continuous and that all beings are dependent on him. Another core teaching found in the Qur'an involves life after death: Muslims believe that at the end of the world, all the dead will be resurrected and judged by

A page from the Qur'an, the sacred scriptures of Islam. Muslims believe that the verses in the Qur'an represent Allah's messages to Muhammad, which he recited and ordered his followers to memorize. The Qur'an was not written down until after Muhammad's death. It is made up of verses and chapters, roughly organized from longest to shortest.

Allah. According to the lives they lived on earth, they will be sent to heaven or hell.

Islam is a religion of laws by which daily life should be conducted. While these laws are elaborated in great detail, and with some variations among the four main schools of Sunni Islam and wider differences in Shia Islam, they are largely similar. The key brief statements of the most important elements are called the "five pillars of Islam." It is crucial that Muslims follow each of these practices. They are:

> A statement of belief called the *Shahada*. It is said in Arabic and states: "I bear witness that there is no god but God, and that Muhammad is His Messenger."
>
> *Salat* (prayer). There are five prayer times each day.

Sawm (fasting). During the month of Ramadan, Muslims are commanded to fast for 30 days during daylight hours.

Zakat (charity). Muslims are told to give a certain percentage of their wealth to charity. *Zakat* should be 2.5 percent of a Muslim's wealth.

Hajj (the pilgrimage to Mecca). All Muslims are obligated to go on *hajj* once in their lifetime as long as they have the money to do so and are physically able.

Another important element of Muhammad's teaching and a central principle of the Qur'an and Islamic law is that of *jihad*. Throughout the history of Islam, jihad has sometimes taken on more limited meanings—an effort to achieve something, including personal betterment. However, the central meaning in the Qur'an and Islamic doctrine has always been that of holy war, or an armed struggle against non-Muslims undertaken in order to spread Islam and to expand *dar al-Islam*, the territory of Islam.

Jihad is so important because undertaking it is considered to be following the example of Muhammad, who during his lifetime fought to spread Islam in Arabia. Therefore, while there are different interpretations of jihad and different ideas about who is permitted to fight, the Qur'an states that jihad is an obligation of all able-bodied Muslim males.

The Hijrah

While some people accepted the message Muhammad was bringing, others in Mecca refused to accept that he was a prophet. Mecca was already a regional religious center because it was the site of the Kaaba, a shrine to Arabian tribal gods that attracted many religious pilgrims. The new religion of Islam was therefore not only spiritually but also economically threatening to many in Mecca because it would undermine the income of people catering to religious pilgrims.

Muslims were persecuted. In 622 Muhammad and his followers left Mecca for a town 200 miles north called Yathrib, which was later renamed Medina. This migration became known as the *hijrah*. The importance of this migration is shown by the fact that the Muslim calendar placed the date of the *hijrah* as its starting year.

The Capture of Mecca

In Medina, Muhammad founded the first Islamic state. Medina was much more tolerant of Islam than Mecca had been, and the

Today, the Prophet's Mosque and surrounding plazas in the modern city of Medina are roughly as large as the entire pre-Islamic city of Yathrib. The city was renamed after the Prophet Muhammad's flight from persecutors in Mecca in 622 C.E. That *hijrah* ("migration") marks the beginning of both the Islamic calendar and the first Islamic state.

religion flourished among the population there. Muhammad founded a community based on Islamic beliefs, combining religious and governmental affairs. However, he still had many enemies, especially among his own tribe, the Quraishis. As the guardians of the Kaaba, the tribe was especially hostile to a religion that denounced its practices as paganism.

Nevertheless, Muhammad was determined to spread his religion, and in 624 he attacked a larger group of Quraishi fighters at the Battle of Badr. Despite being greatly outnumbered, Muhammad and his forces prevailed and killed several top Quraishi leaders. Impressed, some local Arab tribes converted to Islam. After several more battles against the Quraish tribe, Muhammad captured Mecca in 630. As Meccans began converting to Islam, Muhammad destroyed the polytheistic idols in the Kaaba. He dedicated the monument to Islam, a compromise that materially benefited the town since the lucrative pilgrimages continued and even intensified. It has since been the holiest site of the Islamic faith.

While Muhammad is always seen in Islam as a mortal being, he is also held up as the ideal model of a man and of proper behavior. This creates certain problems given his marriage to a nine-year-old girl and his involvement in warfare, torture, and assassination of his enemies. For example, he ordered the murder of Asma bint Marwan, a poet who had been critical of him, and the killing of all male members of the Jewish Khaybar tribe and the selling of all the women and children into slavery after they had surrendered under his promise of fair treatment.

Another problem is that actions legitimized by Muhammad, the Qur'an, and the Sunna (the traditions of early Islam)—which are seen as being ordained by God—cannot be abrogated by later human decisions. Thus, wife-beating (albeit limited in extent), amputation for thefts, and a death sentence for apostasy from

Islam can be ignored by governments or even Muslims but cannot formally be changed in terms that are seen as officially revising Islamic beliefs and practices.

The fact that Muhammad united religious and political power also set a precedent allowing modern-day Islamists to argue that no division could be made between these two spheres and that Islamic religious law must always prevail in governance. These arguments are contradicted by the actual history of Islam—a powerful and often dominating precedent in itself—but on purely doctrinal grounds the Islamists have a case persuasive to many.

During his lifetime, Muhammad was Islam's unquestioned religious as well as political leader. When he died in 632, just two years after the capture of Mecca, the Muslim community had to decide who would succeed him.

The Battle for Leadership and the Sunni-Shia Rift

Upon the death of Muhammad, Islam needed to find a new leader—not a new prophet (as Muhammad was regarded as the last of Allah's prophets) but a political-religious leader, or caliph. The battle for the role of successor went on for many years and irreparably fractured the new religion. This also poses a problem in Islamic doctrine since the early era is designated as a golden age, and the model for Islamists today, yet it was a time of so much violence and instability.

Some Muslims believed that the caliph should be determined by a vote of learned men in the community who should pick the man best suited for the role. In the end a caliph was nominated in this way, and Abu Bakr, one of Muhammad's earliest followers, was chosen.

The group of Muslims who believe this was the correct way to determine successors came to be known as Sunnis.

They believed that according to the Sunna—a collection of sayings (*hadith*) and actions of Muhammad—had never chosen a successor because he wanted this to be determined by the community.

A second group of Muslims thought differently, however. They believed Muhammad had already nominated Ali, his cousin and son-in-law, as caliph. This group became known later as Shia, a word stemming from the term "*shi'at Ali,*" meaning "supporters of Ali." Today about 85 percent of all Muslims are Sunnis, and the conflicts between them and the Shia continue to divide Muslims.

Abu Bakr died in 634 and his chosen successor, Umar ibn al-Khattab (ruled 634–644), became the second caliph. Umar, who had also been one of Muhammad's closest advisers, is best known for overseeing the massive expansion of the Islamic empire.

This shrine to Ali, the fourth caliph, is located near al-Najaf, Iraq. Both Sunni and Shiite Muslims revere Ali as one of the *rashidun*, or "Rightly Guided Caliphs"—Muslim leaders who knew Muhammad and who are said to have ruled according to his teachings.

At this time there were two great empires in the region. To the west of Arabia was the Byzantine Empire; to the east, the Persian Empire. These two rivals had fought long wars with each other and as a result were weakened. High taxes and arbitrary rule had made them unpopular among their subjects.

Umar's forces from Arabia were able to take advantage of this situation. They conquered much of the nearby empires' lands and brought Islam to them in a remarkably short period. In this way, Islam was spread across many countries, including Iraq, much of what is now the Middle East, and North Africa. From North Africa, Muslim forces began to conquer Spain in 711. Umar also established an administration for newly conquered lands and codified Islamic law.

The quick victory over two of the world's greatest empires gave Muslims an even greater sense of confidence that they

The Alhambra was a fortress built by the Moors, Muslims from North Africa who invaded and conquered the Iberian Peninsula (modern-day Spain and Portugal) during the eighth century. The Moorish state was known as al-Andalus, or Andalusia.

enjoyed divine support and that their triumph, at least eventually, would always be assured even against overwhelming odds. They were also determined to incorporate the new lands and peoples not only into their empire but also into their religion.

Non-Muslims were required to pay special taxes and to accept their submissive status, including many restrictions. Christian or Jewish houses of worship could not be built, repaired, or be larger than Islamic mosques. Believers in other religions were forbidden to proselytize among Muslims, while any Muslim converting to another religion would face the punishment of death.

There were many reasons that people in conquered lands converted to Islam. Some became Muslims out of genuine religious conviction; others were interested in the economic, career, or social benefits that conversion would bring. Direct force was more rarely but sometimes used to gain converts. The fate of those who did not become Muslim in conquered lands varied greatly over time and according to the specific Muslim rulers or empires in question.

Within Islam, Christians and Jews are known as *dhimmis*—they are given special status compared with people of other religions because they are "people of the book," possessing monotheistic religious texts that Muslims believe were valid at least in the pre-Islamic era. Freedom to practice their religion is given to *dhimmis* in exchange for submission to Islamic rule. Again, treatment varied widely over time and depending on the rulers. At times, individuals were given great opportunities in the economic sphere and even served as advisers to Muslim rulers. At other times, there was violent, repressive treatment.

The Conquest of Iran

The conquest of Iran was particularly significant in the history of Islam. Iran in the seventh century was largely Zoroastrian and had a strong identity and an advanced culture. The Arab invasion transformed the Persians into Muslims, yet they retained a distinctive cultural identity, which would in turn have a tremendous influence both on Islam and on the Islamic empire.

The conquest of Iran began in 633, when Islamic armies seized the important city of al-Hira. The Muslim general dispatched a letter to local leaders across Iran. "Submit to our authority," it read, "and we shall leave you and your land and go by you against others. If not, you will be conquered against your will by men who love death as you love life."

The second caliph, Umar, pushed the Islamic conquest deep into Iran. Between 641 and 644, the Islamic armies, lured by promises of fiefdoms and booty, conquered most of Iran, expanding the domains of Islam all the way to the Indus River. Although the Iranian shah (king) was gone, the nobility remained. Many from this group converted to Islam, often in order to protect their privileged status under the caliph, who would not accept non-Muslim local rulers. Iran's sense of identity did remain, however, and even those who converted to Islam continued to celebrate traditional Iranian holidays like Nowruz, the Persian New Year.

Of particular importance would be the influence of Persian practices on the intellectual and court life of the Islamic empire during its peak and also on the development of Shia doctrine and the extension of that branch of Islam. Many scholars believe that Shia views had a special appeal to Persians.

Sunnis have particular admiration for Umar as the architect of the great expansion of Islam, including the conquest of Persia. In contrast, Shias have a special loathing for Umar because they believe he denied Ali his birthright as the rightful caliph. In 644, Umar was killed by a non-Muslim Persian slave in Medina. Umar's successor was Uthman. He, too, presided over the

This illustration from a Persian manuscript depicts Muslims making the hajj, or pilgrimage to Mecca. Arab Muslim armies completed their conquest of the Persian Empire by 656 C.E. The Persian civilization was older and more sophisticated, and the Arabs incorporated Persian language, literature, and cultural practices into the expanding Islamic empire.

expansion of the Islamic empire. Uthman was assassinated in 656 by a group of Egyptian rebels. As a result of Uthman's death, Ali was finally awarded the title of caliph. His troubled reign would end with his assassination in 661 by a disgruntled group of former supporters known as the Kharijites.

The first four caliphs are known by Sunnis as "the Rightly Guided Caliphs" and are considered true examples of Islamic leadership. Shias, on the other hand, consider Ali's three predecessors to have been illegitimate rulers. Indeed, in Shia mosques, especially when they are outside the supervision of a Sunni-dominated government, part of the religious service includes the ritual cursing of the first three caliphs.

Ali's Rule and the Rise of the Umayyads

Soon after he became caliph, Ali found himself facing great difficulties. Many Muslims held him responsible for the death of

Uthman. Mu'awiya, a relative of Uthman and the powerful governor of Syria, took the lead in this movement.

This led to the battle at Siffin in July 657. At first, Ali's forces appeared to be winning. But then both sides agreed that the

Shia Groups

The Shia movement is split into three different sects: Twelvers, Ismaili, and Zaidi. The three sects differ, among other ways, in the number of Imams they believe to have come after Ali. (The term *Imams* in this case refers to male descendants of Ali who are said to have been divinely guided Shia leaders.)

Twelvers believe that there were 12 Imams. According to Twelver belief, the 12th Imam disappeared in 874 and is hidden by God until a time in the future when he will reappear to bring absolute justice to the world. Today, about 80 percent of Shias are Twelvers, and there are large communities of them in Iran, Iraq, and Lebanon.

Ismailis (also called Seveners) split with the Twelvers over the identity of the rightful seventh Imam. They believe that the religious authority of the sixth Imam, Jafar al-Sadiq, passed to his son Ismail even though Ismail died before his father. Twelvers believe another son became the rightful Imam upon Jafar's death in 765. Today, there are some 3 million Ismailis divided into two branches. The Mustalian branch is in North Yemen, and the Nizari branch is in Afghanistan, Iran, and parts of India, Pakistan, and East Asia. From the 9th to the 13th century, Ismailis were the dominant power in the Muslim world. The height of their influence came in the 10th century, when an Ismaili Fatimid caliph conquered Egypt.

Zaidis (also called Fivers in the West) recognized the first four Imams but contended that Zaid bin Ali was the fifth. The Zaidis were considered the Shias closest in their beliefs to Sunnis since they did not believe that the Imams were semi-divine or that there was a hidden Imam. Zaidis make up 25 percent of the population of Yemen and are centered in that nation's mountainous northern region.

A Shiite woman carries her child during an Ashura celebration in Kadamiya, Iraq. Shiites celebrate Ashura each year on the tenth day of the Islamic month of Muharram. The solemn festival commemorates the martyrdom of Ali's son Hussein at the Battle of Karbala in 680 C.E.—a battle that marks the permanent division of Islam into Sunni and Shiite factions.

outcome of the battle should be decided by arbitrators using the Qur'an to determine which man had the stronger claim to be caliph.

The outcome of the tribunal was unclear, but in the end Mu'awiya became caliph. He established the Umayyad dynasty, whose triumph was somewhat ironic given that many of its ancestors or founders had been opponents of Muhammad in Islam's earlier days. Mu'awiya made Damascus in Syria the capital of his empire, which now stretched from Egypt in the west to Persia in the east. From Mu'awiya on, the title of caliph became hereditary. Thus, while the political and religious power was combined, the emphasis now went to the political side. The empire had become institutionalized: rather than being a theocracy, religion was a tool of the ruling group.

One of Ali's sons, Hussein, was determined not to give up his family's claim on the caliphate and decided to fight Mu'awiya. Hussein was travelling with a small force of supporters in present-day Iraq when Mu'awiya's army attacked them near Karbala in 680. Hussein was killed along with all his men.

This event is emotionally and psychologically central for the Shia. Hussein's suffering and martyrdom has been commemorated annually in the Shia holiday of Ashura. During this holiday, some Shia men flagellate themselves with swords and chains to symbolize the suffering of Hussein. There is an underlying attitude in Shia Islam of being a persecuted underdog group, and Hussein's death is an important symbol. In contrast, the Sunnis have tended to view themselves as the legitimate ruling group in Islam.

The Abbasid Dynasty

As Islam spread, so did the signs of its presence. Throughout the empire mosques were built in Damascus, Aleppo, Medina, and Jerusalem. In spite of this, the Umayyads were unpopular. The Umayyad caliph and his governors favored Arabs and discriminated against Persians. Umayyad mismanagement also compounded Iranian resentment toward their new leadership. The reaction to this situation was often religious, and Persians flocked to Shiism.

Rise of the Abbasids

The unpopularity of the Umayyads led to revolutions and rebellions within their empire. Most significant was the growing revolution in Khurasan, in eastern Persia. It was led by descendants of Muhammad's uncle al-Abbas; they were known as the Abbasids. In 747 the Abbasids, who used black flags as symbols for their revolution, captured power in Khurasan.

In 750 the Umayyads lost control of the empire to the Abbasids. The Abbasids moved the empire's capital from

The Dome of the Rock is an Islamic shrine built on the ruins of the ancient Jewish Temple in Jerusalem. According to Muslim tradition, it was from this place that Muhammad journeyed to heaven to meet with Moses and other prophets. The Dome and the nearby al-Aqsa Mosque were constructed at the order of the Umayyad caliph in 691 C.E.

Damascus to Baghdad. They were to rule the Islamic world for 500 years, although their power weakened considerably during this period.

The new capital Baghdad was far more Persian than Arab, and Iranian influence increased dramatically. The Abbasids modeled their new administration on that of the Sassanians, the rulers of the pre-Islamic Persian empire. The new caliphs also relied heavily on Iranian expertise, and prosperity returned to Iran during the Abbasid dynasty. However, in spite of this and the fact that both Arabs and Persians were united by Islam, ethnic tensions continued to strain the empire. The caliphs were still Arab, and the Arabs continued to claim a privileged position within the world of Islam, arguing that God had chosen to reveal the Qu'ran in Arabic, not in Persian.

The Abbasids were also at odds with the Shia. During their rise to power, they had relied on the help of the Shia as well as many *Mawali* (non-Arab Muslims). However, once their dynasty was established in Baghdad, the Abbasids became a strong Sunni power, rejecting their Shia alliance. In 786 an uprising in Mecca led to the massacre of many Shia. Survivors fled to the Maghreb, where they established a kingdom know as Idrisid.

This silver coin was minted at Baghdad, capital of the Abbasid empire, around 800 C.E. The Abbasid period is often considered a golden age of Islamic history. It was a time in which Muslim scholars made great advances in chemistry, mathematics, geography, astronomy, and other sciences.

In 813 Ma'mun became caliph of the Abbasid empire. He expanded the bureaucracy and continued to professionalize it along the Iranian model. He was well known for his patronage of the arts and sciences. His 25-year-long reign marked the height of Abbasid rule.

Fragmentation of the Empire

After Ma'mun, Abbasid power began to weaken throughout the empire. Different dynasties and powers took control in different regions. Opposition also grew when the 12th Shia Imam disappeared in 874, leading certain Shia groups to take revenge by attacking Sunni institutions.

In 909 Egypt came under the control of the Fatimids, an Ismaili Shia dynasty that incorporated a number of non-Islamic influences in its religious interpretation. The Fatimids opposed the Sunni Abbassids in Baghdad.

In 1171 the Fatimids were replaced by Salah al-Din (known in the West as Saladin). A military leader, he became one of the most famous Islamic rulers by defeating the European Crusaders. The Crusaders conquered lands in the

This page from a 15th-century manuscript shows European knights fighting Muslim warriors. The Crusades were a series of wars (1095–1291 C.E.) fought between Christians and Muslims for control of the Holy Land.

Levant during the 11th and 12th centuries; their aim was to reestablish Christian rule in their holy lands. Salah al-Din recaptured Jerusalem from the Crusaders in 1187. He also founded a new dynasty known as the Ayyubids, which ruled Egypt until 1252.

In short, the once unified Islamic empire had divided into many local states. The religiously defined direction had been

The Spread of Islam to East Asia and Africa

Although the growth and spread of Islam was a complex process and varied in every place, it often began with trade. As Muslim merchants traveled trade routes, they also brought their religion.

Trade brought Islam to Southeast Asia. There are records of Muslim presence in Malaysia dating from the very first years of the 13th century, though Islam had probably reached the region many years earlier. In the 16th and 17th centuries, as rulers converted to Islam, small Islamic empires grew in Malaysia and Indonesia. Today Indonesia has the largest Muslim population in the world.

Arab and Persian trade (as well as the slave trade across the Indian Ocean) also brought Islam to East Africa. In Somalia, Zanzibar, and Mozambique the religion grew. In West Africa, Islam was also spread by tribes. Islamized Berber tribes from North Africa spread the religion south to Ghana and Mali. In the Sudan, Islam was spread by a complex process of trade, tribes and conquest.

In all these regions Islam was mixed with indigenous culture and religion. For example, in Sudan in the 19th century, against a background of Islamic belief and local political and cultural conditions, a revivalist movement known as Mahdism emerged. It was led by Muhammad Ahmad, who proclaimed himself to be the Mahdi, a messianic figure expected to establish justice near the end of time. He drove out the British and Egyptian authorities for a dozen years before his movement was wiped out.

replaced by political considerations and dynastic interests. Nevertheless, Islam remained a powerful force that shaped these societies.

The rise of local dynasties in western Iran threatened Abbasid rule in Baghdad itself. In the early 10th century, a Shia family from the Caspian Sea area consolidated control over interior Iranian towns such as Karaj, Isfahan, and Shiraz. This Buyid family also moved into Iraq, and in 945 the Buyids seized Baghdad itself. While accepting the titular authority of the Abbasid caliph, the Buyid ruler assumed control as the grand *vazir*. The Buyids, like the Abbasids, traced their line back to the Sassanian Empire; they adopted the ancient pre-Islamic title, *Shahanshah* (meaning "king of kings"). In this way, three centuries after the armies of Islam had swept across the Iranian plateau, traditional Iranian culture remained. The invading Arab armies may have brought a new religion, but Iran sheltered offshoots and spawned new sects of Islam. Judaism, Christianity, and Zoroastrianism remained potent influences as well.

Inventions like the astrolabe (pictured) and improvements to the compass made it easier for Muslims to cross the Indian Ocean. This helped facilitate the spread of Islam into East Africa, Indonesia, and the Philippines.

Seeds of Stagnation

Culturally and religiously, this was also a significant period for the Muslim world. Across the Middle East a flourishing civilization developed. Persians contributed to the development of poetry, historical scholarship, and the study of science. In the Arab world there were important contributions to the development of mathematics, including the invention of algebra.

Yet while the revival of intellectual inquiry and scientific study came earlier in the Islamic world than in the West, it ultimately petered out. Some of the reasons why the Muslim-majority countries fell behind the Western world technologically, politically, militarily, and economically centuries later can be found in the developments of the 11th, 12th, and 13th centuries in the Islamic region.

In the West, nation-states would coalesce and gradually seek legitimacy and stability. Nobles and cities would win institutionalized rights against the monarch. The secular space—or at least the right to free inquiry up to a point—was slowly opened up by scholars and scientists who argued that free inquiry was consistent with their religious beliefs. A reconnection was made with the pre-Christian classical cultures. And later, the Protestant Reformation would open up new social and intellectual vistas. In Europe, people were burned at the stake for their new ideas or dissenting actions, but they laid a basis which would be built upon and eventually produce dramatic changes.

None of these things happened in Muslim-majority societies. Briefly, the reason was the victory of traditionalist-oriented hard-line theologians, not only at the time but in a triumph that continued for many centuries thereafter. If there were Arab philosophers, scientists, and translators in the Middle Ages, few of their Muslim compatriots were ever aware of their work, and it had no lasting influence in their own societies.

In the 11th century, for example, Ibn Salah al-din al Shahrouzi issued a *fatwa* (a legal decree handed down by an Islamic religious leader) banning the study of logic as a "heresy delivering man into Satan's bosom." It is often said that at this time "the gates of *ijtihad*" were closed. *Ijtihad* involves scholars using reasoning to debate and reinterpret religious texts to new times and situations. This was rejected and that stance was enforced by both mosque and state. The emphasis would be on reinforcing traditional rulings and emulating examples of earlier caliphs and judges. In theory, it might be claimed that Islam accepted adjustments to circumstances and innovations, but in practice this rarely happened.

The End of the Abbasids

Meanwhile, the Abbasids in Baghdad were suffering further decline. In 1055 a Turkish dynasty, the Seljuks, conquered Baghdad. These new Sunni rulers did not claim to be caliphs and did not overthrow the Abbasids but simply ruled under the suzerainty of the Abbasids. This development was not only important because of the decline of Abbasid power but also for the change in the nature of power. Before the Seljuks, the caliph held both political and religious power. Now the Seljuk sultan took charge of running the state while the caliphs became simply spiritual rulers. This was a fundamental and lasting change in Islamic rule. It was also significant in that Arabs or even Persians were no longer holding all the power in Muslim lands.

The complete destruction of Abbasid rule came in the 13th century with the Mongol invasions. In 1258 the Mongols—tribes from Mongolia that had been unified by Genghis Khan—captured Baghdad and then abolished the Abbasid caliphate. Later they converted to Islam and ruled over Iran and Iraq until 1336.

The Mongols were not able to conquer Egypt, however. By this time the Mamluks—a group of Turkish military slaves from central Asia imported by the Ayyubids—had seized power. In spite of the Mongol invasions, the Mamluks were able to maintain their rule over Egypt, Syria, and the holy cities of Arabia until 1517.

The Ottoman, Safavid, and Mughal Empires

Three major Islamic empires emerged at the end of the Middle Ages. These empires would dominate the Islamic world for centuries.

The Ottoman Turks

During the 14th century the Ottomans, a Turkish dynasty, grew in Anatolia. The Ottomans created an empire that would stretch from southeastern Europe to Egypt and to the Persian Gulf. By the end of the 14th century the Ottomans had expanded into the Balkans. Under Mehmed II, they conquered Constantinople, capital of the Byzantine Empire, in 1453. The city was renamed Istanbul and became the Ottoman capital. A decade later Bosnia was also conquered. In 1516–17, the Ottomans defeated the Mamluks and absorbed Syria, Egypt, and western Arabia into their empire.

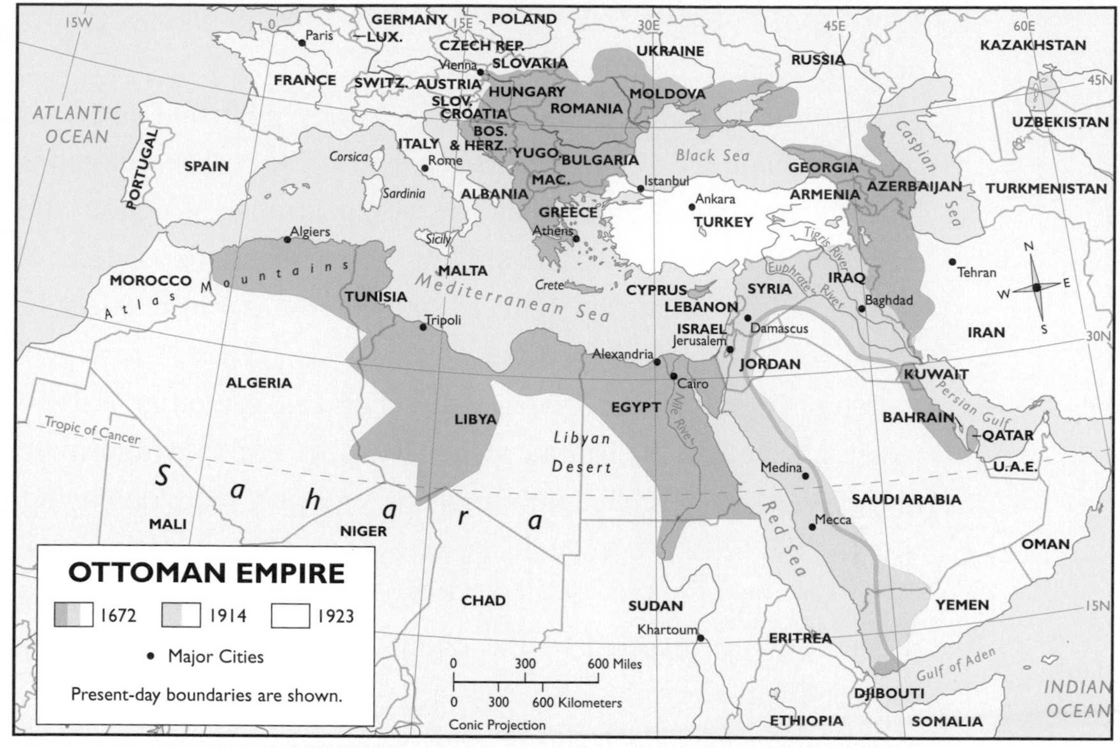

The powerful Ottoman Empire was based in the Anatolian Peninsula (modern-day Turkey). At its height in 1672 the empire controlled vast territories in the Middle East, North Africa, Central Asia, and Eastern Europe. By the start of World War I (1914), however, imperial rule was concentrated in the Middle East. After the war, the Ottoman territories were divided among the victorious Allied powers (particularly France, Great Britain, and Italy), and the secular state of Turkey was created (1923).

During the campaign against the Mamluks, the Ottomans adopted the title of caliph for their leader, thus making their empire a successor to that originally founded by Muhammad. Islamic legitimacy was an important element in the Ottomans' standing with their mostly non-Turkish subjects. As the defenders of Sunni Islam, they protected and organized pilgrimages to Muslim holy sites. The state upheld Sharia law throughout the empire, with *qadi*, religious judges of the Hanafi school, appointed to ensure its implementation. Under Sultan Suleyman I (known as "Suleyman the Magnificent"), who ruled from 1520 to

1566, the Ottoman Empire reached the height of its cultural achievement.

By the 18th century, Ottoman military and political power was on the decline. The empire began to lose territory. The Ottomans had originated a relatively efficient administrative structure and army, including the forcible drafting and conversion of tens of thousands of Balkan Christians as soldiers. But dynastic quarrels, weak sultans, and—beginning in the 19th century—forces of nationalism within the empire led to decline. Another issue—which affected all the Islamic states—was the rapid advancement of the West. But equally important, and probably more damaging, was the failure of the Muslim countries to achieve such progress.

Of all the Muslim-ruled states, however, the Ottomans tried the hardest to respond to the challenge of the West, starting especially in the mid-19th century with internal reforms, the study of Europe's institutions, education, and military reorganization. These efforts were limited and failed to overcome the tremendous barriers to success.

There were three main lines of strategy proposed in the late 19th century for saving the gradually retreating and declining

A squad of Ottoman cavalry, circa 1890. By the late 19th century, the Ottoman Empire was struggling to maintain control over its far-flung territories. The sultans were forced to rely on European powers like Great Britain and France for financial and military help.

The Taj Mahal, built during the 17th century by a Muslim ruler in Agra, India, is considered one of the world's greatest architectural accomplishments.

empire. Some advocated a pan-Islamic ideology, tying together the empire's subjects by religion, a potent tactic over the centuries but useless in its non-Muslim European provinces. Others focused on Ottomanism, trying to muster loyalty for the multiethnic, multireligious empire.

The eventual winners, however, were the third group: the Turkish nationalists, whose program of revitalization centered on rallying the Turks as the empire's ruling group. In 1908 a group of reformers called the Young Turks led a revolt against the sultan. Aside from increasing friction with the non-Turks, this effort was scuttled by the Ottoman Empire's entry into World War I on the German side. The British backed an Arab nationalist revolt and defeated Ottoman armies. This defeat marked the empire's end.

Wahhabism

In the 18th century an extremely conservative form of Islam emerged in Saudi Arabia. It was developed by a religious scholar named Muhammad ibn Abd al-Wahhab, who preached that only the purest form of Sunni Islam was acceptable. Al-Wahhab dismissed all other forms of Islam, such as Sufism and Shiism, being especially hostile to the latter. He also condemned and tried to destroy all forms of *shirk* (idolatry), which he believed was threatening Islam at the time.

Al-Wahhab forged an alliance with Muhammad ibn Saud, the patriarch of a powerful family in central Arabia. In the 20th century, a descendant of Ibn Saud's would unify Arabia and establish the state of Saudi Arabia. Wahhabism was adopted as the official form of Islam in Saudi Arabia. It is Wahhabi ideology that has led to the extremely strict Islamic laws there.

Former Ottoman territories either became fully independent or came under British or French control.

In 1923, the Turkish republic was formed by Kemal Ataturk, who made it a secular state. The following year, the caliphate was abolished. This was a truly historic moment. Although the caliphate had long since changed from what had existed at the time of the first four caliphs, it was still a symbol of Islamic unity. Now that symbol was gone, a development that was emblematic of the triumph of nationalism over religious loyalty as the glue holding together Middle Eastern states. Today, the reestablishment of the caliphate is a major demand among radical Islamists.

The Safavids

The Safavid dynasty ruled Iran from 1501 to 1722. Their beginnings are connected to a Sufi order originally led by Shaikh

Safi al-Din (1252–1334). The order grew in importance and was influential in the Mongol Empire. When Ismail became head of the order, he proclaimed himself shah in 1501—the year scholars generally point to as the start of the Safavid

Sufism

Sufis are Islamic mystics. Most early Sufis were Arabs. But during the Abbasid period, as the center of the Islamic world shifted eastward, Persia came to play a greater role in the Sufi community. The center of Sufism slowly gravitated from Baghdad and Basra to Khurasan, which consequently became known as "the land whose product is saints."

Sufi practice varies enormously. It can involve philosophy, special spiritual practices that are meant to bring the believer closer to God, and strict adherence to sharia.

Sufis are organized within *tariqahs*, or orders. They are headed by shaikhs. Some of the most famous Persian poetry, which is still studied today, was written in the 13th century by Sufi mystics like Rumi, 'Attar, and Saadi.

Turkish Sufis, known as dervishes, perform a whirling dance that they believe brings them into close contact with Allah.

Empire. Safavid rule is important in the history of Islam as well as of Iran since Ismail proclaimed Twelver Shiism as the empire's official religion.

Sunni Legal Schools

When compared with the Shia, Sunnis show considerably more unanimity. They do have four different schools of legal interpretation, but these coexist easily. Each of the schools is named after its founding jurist, who differed in how he interpreted the sharia, or Islamic law. Interpreting sharia was an increasingly difficult task because of changing conditions over time. The legal schools developed around the time of the Abbasid dynasty.

Hanafi. This is the largest school and also the oldest. Its followers are in Afghanistan, Turkey, Iraq, Syria, and Egypt. Hanafi Islam is relatively liberal. It is open to differences among Muslims and stresses that a Muslim's belief is more important than how he or she practices.

Maliki. The second-largest Sunni legal school, Maliki is common in North Africa, including parts of Egypt.

Shafi. This school has the easiest personal rules to follow. It is popular in parts of southern Arabia, Lower Egypt, and among Syrians, Palestinians, and most Kurds in Iraq.

Hanbali. The smallest school, Hanbali is often referred to in the West as Wahhabi Islam. Hanbali is the strictest Sunni legal school and tends to be more intolerant to the others. Its followers constitute the great majority of people in Saudi Arabia and Qatar.

Despite the differences in the four legal schools, Sunni Muslims generally consider them all equally valid.

While there had always been a strong Shia presence in Iran, Sunnis had remained supreme. The adoption of Shiism had important consequences for Iran. First, it gave Iranians a national identity, which differentiated them from Ottoman subjects. Second, it gave Shiism a power base that would ensure survival and provide a significant influence in the years to come. This event led many Sunnis to flee Iran. Jews were also oppressed, and many fled to Ottoman lands. Despite the discrimination and outright oppression, it took a couple of centuries for Ismail's plan to be fully implemented.

The Mughals

At its height, the Mughal Empire (1526–1858) stretched across most of India. The empire was ruled by a Sunni dynasty established by Babur, a descendant of the Mongol leader Timur (known in the West as Tamerlane).

In many ways India—then as now a predominantly Hindu land—flourished under the rule of the Muslim Mughals. Babur and other Mughal emperors adopted certain Hindu customs and practices in order to facilitate their rule. However, the Mughal era also saw repression of Hindus; at times, large numbers of Hindus were killed or forcibly converted to Islam.

The Mughals' cultural achievements are undeniable. Under their rule, great works of art and magnificent architectural wonders were created. These include, most famously, the Taj Mahal. Located at Agra, it was built in the 17th century by the Mughal emperor Shah Jahan as a monument to his favorite wife.

The Mughal Empire came to an end when the British Crown took control of India in 1858. In 1947 the British withdrew from India, which was partitioned into the predominantly Hindu (but secular) state of India, and the Muslim state of Pakistan.

Islam in the Modern World

Islam continues to expand in the modern world, but the modern world has also presented the religion with many problems. Muslims have had to ask how Islam should be practiced in the 20th and 21st centuries. Should Islam be adapted to modern conditions, or should Muslims seek to preserve the Islam of Muhammad's time and reject the changes of the modern world? During the 20th century, three main Islamic approaches to the modern world came to the fore: conservative-traditionalism, modernism, and Islamism.

Conservative-Traditionalism

Conservative-traditionalism has been for centuries—and remains—the mainstream of Islam in the modern world. Put very simply, it involves the status quo. The political system is accepted as it is, while adherents follow Islamic law to a large extent based on their personal preference but also taking into account familial and social pressure, which varies among countries, sectors of society, and families. Conservative-traditionalist Muslims may sympathize with Islamist groups or even terrorism but do not want such movements to take power in their own country.

They neither reject the current life in their own country nor seek to modernize or reform Islam as it is practiced. They respect government-sponsored clerics and official religious institutions. Obviously, this is a more complex matter in places ruled by Islamists—notably Iran and the Gaza Strip—but there are many who regard themselves as pious Muslims who do not support these regimes and there are millions of such people who endorse Arab nationalism or communal nationalist groups.

Indonesian Muslims prepare for a prayer service in a mosque on the island of Sumatra. In countries like Indonesia, most people are conservative-traditionalist Muslims.

A useful example of the difference between conservative-traditional Islam and Islamism is that followers of the former are more likely to favor a constitutional provision in their countries that Islamic law is a source of legislation, while Islamists would demand that it be the sole source of legislation. At the same time, Islamist pressure can alter its rival. In the past, suicide in committing an act of terrorism against anyone would be deemed quite un-Islamic, while today leading clerics, though not all, find it legitimate, though they might limit the targets.

Still, given the power of this stream, Islamists find it harder to build a majority base of support or take over countries, while modernists find little sympathy at all.

Modernism

In the late 19th and early 20th century, some Muslim intellectuals looked at Europe and saw the dramatic contrast with their own societies. Europe was industrializing, advancing technologically and militarily. Its power and influence was spreading all over the world. In contrast, Muslim countries remained weak and undeveloped. One of the first dramatic examples of this occurred in 1798 when Napoleon and his French forces easily seized Egypt, which was ruled by local soldiers though nominally under Ottoman suzerainty.

Napoleon's 1798 capture of Egypt forced leaders in the Muslim world to admit that their civilization had fallen behind Europe technologically. This led to a modernization movement among Muslims during the 19th and 20th centuries.

From this point on there were movements within the Muslim world that sought to understand why the West had become so powerful and to find ways that the Islamic world could compete. One important solution was the idea that Islam should adapt to the modern world so that it would once again be able to flourish.

Two key figures who asked why their societies were lagging behind and what could be done about it were Muhammad Abduh (1849–1905) and Rashid Rida (1865–1935). Abduh wanted to demonstrate that while Islam followed God's will and could not fundamentally be changed, the Qur'an also contained social principles that had to be interpreted and applied to the current time. Only through this conciliation of Islam to the modern world could Muslims survive within it.

Similarly, Rida, who lived for most of his life in Cairo, was troubled by why Muslims seemed to be so weak when faced with the great European powers. He contended that certain economic, educational, and political practices from Europe could be adopted at the same time that Muslims returned to the true essence of Islam. Rida also wanted to see the caliphate rebuilt.

Yet even at the start some of the weaknesses in the modernist argument could be seen. First, it was expressed by relatively isolated intellectuals without organizational skills or a mass base of support. Second, they had to put great emphasis on the idea that their plans would strengthen, rather than weaken, Islam. Yet critics could easily argue—using European history and experience in their own countries—that modernization reduced the power of religion. Third, the modernists had to insist on the sacredness of Islam and all its basic precepts, so opponents could quote traditional texts and generally accepted clerics to defend anti-reform views and the forbidden nature of such changes. Finally, the modernist case appealed only to those already possessing at least a partly Western education, a small minority.

The work of these early modernists eventually lost out to what became a far more powerful ideology. By the 1950s, Arab nationalism became the dominant ideology. Populist dictatorship rather than Islamic reform was extolled as the way to achieve unity and progress. While elements in Arab nationalism—particularly the Baath Party, which ruled in Syria and Iraq—evinced leftist secularist notions, such ideas were quickly dropped, as pushing them would prompt massive popular opposition.

In reaction to the perceived failures of the Arab nationalist regime and the threat of radical Islamism, a new wavelet of reform-minded Muslim thinkers developed in the late 20th and early 21st centuries. This was especially true in Asian countries. A notable example was Abdurrahman Wahid, head of Indonesia's largest Muslim organization and then the country's president from 1999 to 2001. Arguably, Indonesia had long been the country with the highest proportion of moderate Muslims in the world. Wahid advocated peaceful relations among religions and democracy. Yet such voices proposing an explicit and systematic reform program remained few.

During the 1950s and 1960s, nationalist leaders like Egypt's Gamal Abdel Nasser (center) gained support in many Arab countries.

Arab nationalists like Muammar al-Qadhafi of Libya (above) and Saddam Hussein of Iraq (at right) drew the ire of Islamists.

Another factor was the influence of Western immigrant Muslim communities. A well-known and controversial new voice was Tariq Ramadan, grandson of the founder of the paradigmatic Islamist group in the 1930s, the Egyptian Muslim Brotherhood. But while Ramadan often spoke in mild terms to Western non-Muslim audiences about the need for Muslims to adapt to being a minority in European countries, he also held some quite radical views, or at least avoided critical issues when addressing Muslims.

The problem remains that while reformist Muslims receive tremendous publicity in the West and their moderate credentials are often exaggerated, they have little influence among large numbers of Muslims and virtually no well-organized movements.

Islamism

Even in the early 21st century, however, reformist voices found it impossible to compete with Islamism. While seeking to return to a time when Islam was not only religion but government, Islamism is a modern phenomenon. It is a response to several factors: the growth and perceived failure of nationalism, the continued gap between Muslim-majority countries and the West, and the introduction of Western ideas and practices. Islamism poses as a response to what is wrong with the Muslim world and how it can be repaired. This is a concept often expressed in the slogan "Islam is the answer."

The views of Islamists vary among movements and countries. But it is possible to broadly define Islamism. Islamism is one interpretation of Islam that is a response to the modern age. Most important, it is not just concerned with religion in the narrow sense but has a political goal: to seize state power and transform society. It is a revolutionary political ideology, parallel to such systematic programs as communism and fascism, liberal democracy and nationalism.

At the core of Islamism is the belief that Islam provides all the elements, structures, and solutions needed by contemporary society. Therefore, Islam should be the commanding source of ideas and laws because humans have no right to choose their systems or laws because God has done so for them. Their job is merely to submit to God's will, which is after all the basis for the name of Islam itself.

Islamists only accept a strict view of Islam based on their interpretation of Muhammad's teachings and very early Islam. The period of the four Rightly Guided Caliphs and the expansion of Islam is considered to be the golden age. Islam's success at the time is taken as proof that it was divinely sanctioned, while modern-day declines are attributed to straying from proper Islamic practice.

Because of this strict interpretation of Islamism, Islamists believe that almost all states where Muslims live are currently

Islamists believe that Muslim societies must be transformed to conform to their traditional, conservative interpretation of the Qur'an.

not adhering to the correct Islam and are in a state of *jahiliyya*. This implies that the majority of clerics are not practicing or teaching Islam properly, and therefore Muslim countries must be thoroughly purged and transformed.

Conservative-traditional Islam accepted all those professing to be Muslim as legitimate in their practice except for very explicit and clear deviations. The country's leader must be a Muslim, but his piety would not be strictly examined. Many of the caliphs of the Islamic empires in medieval times were quite clearly ready to break Islamic laws (for example, by drinking alcohol). *Takfir* is the practice of declaring someone who is a Muslim to be in fact an unbeliever. Since apostasy from Islam is punishable by death, *takfir* implies that it is proper to kill such people. It thus can authorize jihad against Muslims as well as those of other religions.

Today, the great majority of Muslims accept the idea that jihad means a struggle against non-Muslims to increase the area under the rule of Islam. But they had for many years treated it as an archaic concept, something not suitable for the modern world. In contrast, Islamists seek to use jihad to mobilize revolutionary forces for violent struggle. They have stressed jihad to be the duty of every Muslim at the present time. While this is often presented in defensive terms, in practice it means offensive warfare. Many conservative-traditionalist Muslims agree, since Islamists have a strong case for this based on the accepted sources.

In short, Islamism is a political ideology that seeks to seize state power and transform existing Muslim-majority societies. It also seeks to fight other countries (including the United States and Israel) deemed to be aggressors on the lands of Islam. Islamism further states that the answer to the problems of the countries where Muslims live is not nationalism, the reform of Islam, or the adoption of Western principles, but only the rule of a strictly interpreted version of Islam.

Islamism blames all the problems of Muslim countries on the West, on Israel, or on Muslims who collaborate with the

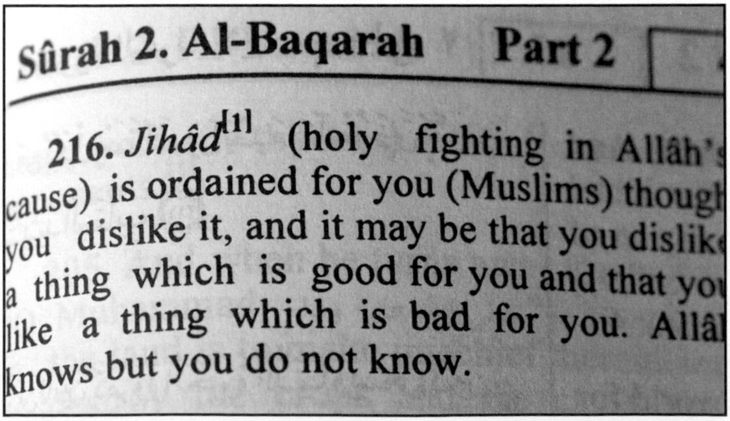

Sûrah 2. Al-Baqarah Part 2

216. *Jihâd*[1] (holy fighting in Allâh's cause) is ordained for you (Muslims) though you dislike it, and it may be that you dislike a thing which is good for you and that you like a thing which is bad for you. Allâh knows but you do not know.

Islamists use the concept of jihad, outlined in Qur'an 2:216 and elsewhere in the Muslim scriptures, to justify attacks against non-Muslims.

West or Israel. Islamists therefore demand the rejection of Western political and cultural influences (though not all technological ones). They also demand the destruction of Israel.

Beyond this, however, Islamism takes many different forms and employs many tactics. There are both Sunni and Shia Islamists (who, while sharing a similar cause, may hate or even kill one another, as in contemporary Iraq). While many Islamist movements have embraced armed struggle and terrorism, they may also be involved in grassroots organizing, social welfare projects, and even elections. In some cases—notably in Jordan and Egypt—Islamists operate within the system, though this may also be only as long as they believe this to be advantageous and fear repression if they escalate their struggle.

Although many Islamist groups exist, three important examples of Islamism are presented here: the Muslim Brotherhood, the Iranian Revolution, and the Islamism of Osama bin Laden.

The Muslim Brotherhood

Islamism as a modern political organization can be traced to the founding of the Egyptian Muslim Brotherhood, by Hassan al-Banna, in 1928. The movement sought to put Egypt under a regime based on Islamic law.

The Brotherhood engaged in assassinations and in 1949 al-Banna was killed by Egyptian government agents. The Muslim Brotherhood then attempted to assassinate the Egyptian president, Gamal Abdel Nasser, after that Arab nationalist took power. Nasser harshly suppressed the Brotherhood during the 1950s.

At this time, Sayyid Qutb became the most important ideologue in the Muslim Brotherhood. His political outlook was in part formed by a visit to the United States. After his time there, he wrote of his contempt for American society and its lack of morality, culture and religion.

Qutb developed the idea that contemporary societies in Muslim countries were comparable to the pre-Islamic era of jahiliyya and were thus illegitimate. He was therefore able to redefine jihad not merely as a struggle to spread Islam to non-Muslim lands but as a struggle to revolutionize and purify countries already Muslim. Qutb was executed by Nasser's government in 1966.

In the 1950s and 1960s, while Arab nationalism dominated many countries, the role of Islam in politics was through its conservative-traditionalist version seeking to preserve the status quo against radical change. However, radical Islamist movements were also developing, notably branches of the Muslim Brotherhood among Syrians, Jordanians, and Palestinians. While the Egyptian, Syrian, and Jordanian Brotherhoods were all strongly anti-Israel and anti-Western, their main focus was on what they called the "near enemy"—that is, Arab governments. Among Palestinians, the Brotherhood gave rise to the Hamas movement, which engaged in terrorism against Israel, and at times attacked the Palestinian nationalist Fatah movement, seizing power from it in the Gaza Strip.

The tactics of the local groups varied depending on the situation. The Muslim Brotherhood does not focus simply on armed struggle but views the revolutionary process as a long-term one, involving building a mass base by providing social services, educating and indoctrinating young people through institutions, using elections, compromising at times with Arab governments, and showing restraint to avoid government repression.

As Sunni groups, the Muslim Brotherhoods have generally been hostile to Shia and to Iran. Hamas, however, has drifted into the Iranian orbit and is also sponsored by Syria.

The Iranian Revolution

In 1979, following almost a year of demonstrations and violence, the shah of Iran, Mohammad Reza Pahlavi, was ousted in a revolution. Many diverse elements of Iranian society had helped to topple him, but it was Ayatollah Ruhollah Khomeini and his Islamist allies who consolidated power. Iran was thus transformed into a Shia Islamist state.

According to Khomeini, there existed a worldwide struggle between the forces of Islam and those of corrupt materialism. Every Muslim, he said, must take sides and must be mobilized to fight the West and also to overthrow regimes in all other Muslim-majority countries, which did not in his view uphold the true way of Islam. The appeal of this revolutionary Islam was also enhanced by the fact that at this time Arab nationalism was becoming increasingly discredited by its failures. If Islamists in Iran could seize power, those in other countries argued, victory was possible and perhaps the Iranians held the secret of success.

The Ayatollah Khomeini (1902–1989) established the modern world's first Islamist state in Iran.

Khomeini, like other Islamists, proclaimed that Islam provides a total way of life, political system, and social organization. He also preached the importance of exporting the revolution. He insisted that this was the only way to follow the example of Muhammad who had, he said, "launched an armed struggle and established a government. He then sent missionaries and representatives everywhere. . . . He brought the glad tidings that we are going to conquer the entire world and destroy everybody. . . . [Muhammad] set up a government and we should do the same. He defended Islam, we should also defend it."

One distinctive factor in Khomeini's view was the rule of a cleric whose knowledge of God's will was so extensive that he would reign correctly. Other Islamist groups were often led by men whose qualifications as religious scholars were quite limited by the standards of conservative-traditionalist Islam. Another key point was the Shia nature of the revolution, which made it unpalatable to many—but by no means to all—Sunnis.

As president of the Islamic Republic of Iran, Mahmoud Ahmadinejad has ignored the international community's criticism of Iran's nuclear program. Ahmadinejad claims that the program is for peaceful purposes, but the United States and other countries fear Iran is attempting to develop a nuclear weapon that it could use to threaten its Arab neighbors or Israel.

Although Iran has remained under Islamist rule, it has not lived up to Khomeini's expectations. Mohammad Khatami, who was president of Iran from 1997 to 2005, favored the survival of Islamist Iran, but on terms quite contrary to what the hard-liners who really ruled the country or their would-be imitators elsewhere wanted, though he was powerless to change anything. Even under hard-line president Mahmoud Ahmadinejad, Iran remains rife with divisions.

In the end the experience of living under an Islamist regime was the most effective factor in convincing people to oppose Islamism. Yet given the power of the regime and its willingness to use force, rig elections, and use its propaganda and economic institutions effectively, the majority is unable to change the system.

Osama bin Laden and al-Qaeda

By the late 1990s, most traditional Muslims still rejected radical Islamism. And while more of its ideas were infiltrating into their thinking, the movement could be judged a failure at that point. Uprisings in Egypt and Algeria had been defeated, and Islamist groups continued to be repressed by governments. While Lebanese and Palestinian Islamist groups could claim successes in individual attacks against Israel, this had not brought them any closer to defeating the Jewish state or gaining leadership over their own peoples.

Moreover, in their attempts to overthrow regimes, radical Islamists attacked, fought, and killed fellow Muslims. This did nothing to enhance their popularity among Muslims. Finally, Islamist groups were very divided and competed among themselves. In short, the Islamist revolution was apparently not succeeding so far.

It was at this moment that Osama bin Laden built al-Qaeda to revitalize the movement. Rather than looking to Iran as a model for Islamism or focusing on revolution against local regimes, bin Laden drew inspiration from events in distant Afghanistan and made attacking the "far enemy" of America and the West his priority.

In the midst of the Cold War, the Soviet Union invaded Afghanistan in 1979 to back a Communist coup there. Afghans supported by foreign Muslim volunteers, armed by the United States and financed by Saudi Arabia, fought a long guerrilla war against the Soviet army and its local allies. The Islamist fighters, known as the mujahedin (those who wage holy war), overthrew the Communist regime after Soviet forces finally pulled out of the country in early 1989. In 1996, a new radical movement, the Taliban, took power in Afghanistan, transforming it into an Islamist state and making it a safe base for foreign Islamists.

Osama bin Laden, a wealthy Saudi, had participated in the struggle against the Soviets. He saw that in fighting non-Muslim Westerners, the Islamists had gained popularity. Bin Laden was convinced that instead of putting the priority on attacking and overthrowing Arab regimes, Islamists should focus on killing Christians and Jews, Westerners and Israelis. In 1988 he had founded al-Qaeda as an international Islamist coalition, spread by Muslims returning from Afghanistan to their various home countries.

This propaganda poster was used to recruit Muslims into Osama bin Laden's al-Qaeda organization. It was discovered by American special forces operating in eastern Afghanistan during Operation Enduring Freedom, 2002.

In 1998 bin Laden announced the creation of an "International Islamic Front for Jihad Against the Jews and Crusaders." Bin Laden's new organization called on all Muslims "to kill the Americans and their allies—civilians and military" which he said "is an individual duty for every Muslim who can do it in any country in which it is possible to do it, in order to liberate the al-Aqsa Mosque [in Jerusalem] and the holy mosque [Mecca] from their grip, and in order for their

A New York City firefighter calls for help as he works in the rubble of the World Trade Center, September 2001. The deadly September 11 terrorist attack on America raised concerns about Islamist organizations like al-Qaeda.

armies to move out of all the lands of Islam, defeated and unable to threaten any Muslim."

It was this ideology that led to the attacks on the United States of September 11, 2001. Al-Qaeda terrorists flew two hijacked jetliners into New York City's World Trade Center and one into the Pentagon. A fourth hijacked plane crashed in a field in Pennsylvania. In all, almost 3,000 people were killed.

In its own narrowly organizational terms, al-Qaeda's offensive was a failure. The organization was driven out of Afghanistan while its Taliban hosts were overthrown by a U.S.-led invasion. Al-Qaeda's movements in Iraq and Saudi Arabia were defeated.

Nevertheless, the attacks contributed to the revitalization of radical Islamism to the benefit of other groups. Gaining strength were the Shia group Hizballah in Lebanon; Hamas among the Palestinians; and Iraqi insurgents, sponsored by Iran among the Shia, and by Syria (with private Saudi financing) among the Sunni. In Egypt, the Muslim Brotherhood did well in elections. Armed movements developed to stage terrorist attacks in countries as far afield as Indonesia, the Philippines, Somalia, and Thailand.

In every Muslim-majority country, Islamism had become the main rival of nationalism. While it did not seize power outside Iran, except in the Gaza Strip and to some extent in Sudan, the movement seemed set to continue fighting for many decades to come.

Conclusion

Islamism is unlikely to triumph. For while in theory all Muslims accept Islam as the proper organizing principle for their lives and societies, the great majority reject the Islamist interpretation of their religion and are horrified by the idea of living under an extremist Muslim society.

Yet reform movements remain very weak, the province of a few isolated intellectuals and clerics. Only in Turkey has an Islamic-oriented but largely non-Islamist party emerged to capture power in elections. There was relatively more reform activity among new Muslim communities in the West, though even there the other two versions predominated.

Islam from its roots in the desert of Arabia is today a truly global religion. Although united by religion, Muslims throughout the world from the Middle East to Europe and from Russia to Southeast Asia and Africa have very different histories, traditions, and cultures. From its beginnings and throughout its expansion, Islam has had to meet the challenges posed by new regions and new times.

Muslims perform one of their five prescribed prayers during an outdoor community gathering.

Today Muslims are also faced with the question of the way to practice Islam in the modern world. There are those who believe Islam should isolate itself from all changes and keep closely to the Islam of Muhammad's time. Others believe that Islam should be adapted to the modern world and modern times. There are Muslims who believe that governments should be Islamic and that Muslims should live under Islamic law, whereas many more believe religion is a private matter and each individual should practice it as he or she sees fit.

Whatever the answers that are reached, these are not new questions but ones that have been asked throughout the history of Islam. At any rate, the battle over interpreting and leading Islam will be one of the main features of 21st-century history.

Chronology

570: Muhammad is born in Mecca.

610: The first revelation of the Qur'an to Muhammad.

622: Muhammad and his followers migrate to Yathrib (now Medina). The move becomes known as the *hijrah*.

624: The Battle of Badr.

630: Muhammad captures Mecca.

632: Muhammad dies and Abu Bakr becomes the first caliph. The start of the expansion of Islam beyond Arabia.

633: Arab armies begin to conquer Iran.

634: Abu Bakr dies and is succeeded by the second caliph, Umar.

644: Umar is killed, and Uthman becomes the third caliph.

656: Uthman is assassinated and Ali becomes the fourth caliph.

657: Battle of Siffin between Ali and Mu'awiya. Ali is later assassinated and Mu'awiya becomes the first Umayyad caliph in Damascus.

680: Hussein, Ali's son and Muhammad's grandson. is killed at Karbala.

750: The Abbasid dynasty is established, with its capital in Baghdad.

813: Ma'mun becomes caliph, marking the peak of Abbasid rule.

909: The Fatimids establish dynasty in Egypt.

945: The Buyids seize control of Baghdad.

1055: The Seljuks conquer Baghdad.

1171: Salah al-Din defeats the Fatimids and establishes a new dynasty, the Ayyubids.

1187: Salah al-Din recaptures Jerusalem from the Crusaders.

1258: The Mongols capture Baghdad and abolish the Abbasid caliphate.

1453: The Ottomans conquer Constantinople (Istanbul), which becomes the capital of the new Islamic empire.

1501: Safavid rule of Iran begins; Twelver Shiism is proclaimed the religion of Iran.

1516–17: The Ottomans absorb Syria, Egypt, and western Arabia into their empire.

1526: The Mughal Empire is established in India.

1923: The Ottoman Empire ends.

1924: The caliphate is abolished.

1928: The Muslim Brotherhood is founded by Hassan al-Banna.

1979: The Iranian Revolution.

1988: Osama bin Laden forms al-Qaeda.

2001: On September 11, al-Qaeda terrorists fly two hijacked jetliners into New York City's World Trade Center and one into the Pentagon; a fourth hijacked plane crashes in Pennsylvania. In all, some 3,000 people are killed.

Glossary

caliph—a successor to Muhammad who was originally both the religious and political leader of Muslims. It later became only a religious title until the position was abolished in 1924.

dhimmis—the term used in Islam for the "people of the book" (Jews and Christians).

fatwa—a legal decree handed down by an Islamic religious leader.

hadith—a collection of the sayings and actions of Muhammad.

hijrah—the migration of Muhammad and his followers from Mecca to Medina in 622.

ijtihad—an Islamic tenet (abandoned in the Middle Ages) in which qualified scholars could interpret Muslim law and tradition through analysis and logic.

Islamism—a political ideology that seeks to attain state power in order to create a society in which Islam, according to the interpretation of the movement, is supreme in all matters.

jahiliyya—the state of paganism and "ignorance" that was traditionally said by Muslims to characterize pre-Islamic societies but that Islamists now say also characterizes contemporary Muslim societies, which they view as insufficiently pious.

jihad—a holy war against non-Muslims.

Qur'an—Islam's holy scriptures, a key source of Islamic law and practice.

Rightly Guided Caliphs—the term used by Sunnis to refer to the first four successors of Muhammad.

sharia—Islamic law.

Shia—the smaller of Islam's two major branches, whose rift with the larger Sunni branch originated with seventh-century disputes over who should succeed Muhammad as leader of the Muslim community.

shirk—idolatry.

Sufism—a form of Islamic mysticism.

Sunna—a collection of accepted practice in Islam, based on the life of Muhammad.

Sunni—a Muslim belonging to the orthodox, majority branch of Islam.

takfir—the labeling of other Muslims as heretics and pagans, often to justify attacks on them.

Wahhabism—an extremely conservative form of Islam, dominant in Saudi Arabia and Qatar, that insists on a literal interpretation of the Qur'an and regards all people with different views, including Muslims, as enemies of Islam.

Further Reading

Esposito, John L., ed. *Oxford Encyclopedia of the Modern Islamic World.* New York: Oxford University Press, 2001.

Gibb, H.A. R., and J.H. Kramers, eds. *Concise Encyclopedia of Islam.* Boston: Brill Academic Publishers, 2001.

Humphreys, Stephen R. *Islamic History: a Framework for Inquiry.* Princeton, N.J.: Princeton University Press, 1991.

Lapidus, Ira M. *History of Islamic Societies.* New York: Cambridge University Press, 2002.

Internet Resources

http://www.fpri.org/

The Web site of the Foreign Policy Research Institute.

http://www.pbs.org/wgbh/pages/frontline/shows/muslims

This Web site from the PBS program *Frontline* examines contemporary Islam through profiles of and interviews with Muslims in the United States, Africa, the Middle East, and Asia.

http://www.fordham.edu/halsall/sbook1d.html

The Internet Medieval Sourcebook provides translations of important Islamic documents from the period.

Index

Numbers in ***bold italics*** refer to captions.